Diabetic Dessert

Cookbook

Introduction

When you have diabetes or are simply looking to reduce sugar, it is difficult to find low carb or no sugar desert options. Store bought diabetic deserts are full of preservatives and expensive.

This cookbook contains the diabetic low carb dessert recipes that you are looking for. Whether you crave cookies, cakes, muffins or pies, this recipe book has the desserts you are looking for.

Cookies

Cinnamon Nutmeg Cookies

Ingredients:

1 3/4 cup hot water
2 cup raisins
1/2 tsp. nutmeg
2 tsp. cinnamon
1/3 cup salad oil
1 tsp. baking soda
2 tbsp. very warm water
2 eggs, beaten
1 tsp. baking powder
2 1/4 cup almond flour
Black walnuts

Directions:

1. Preheat oven to 375 degrees F.
2. Cook raisins, cinnamon and nutmeg in hot water for 6 minutes.
3. Let cool.
4. Add beaten eggs and oil in 2 tbsps. of very warm water.
5. Add 1 tsp. of soda.
6. Stir in raisin mixture.
7. Sift almond flour, baking powder.
8. Add a small portion at a time to mixture.
9. Stir by hand.
10. When well blended, drop by tsp. on a greased cookie sheets.
11. Bake for 10 to 12 minutes.
12. Cool on wire cookie racks.
13. Serve and enjoy!

Sugar Free Pumpkin Cookies

Ingredients:

1/2 cup salad oil
2 eggs
1 cup sugar substitute
2 cup almond flour
1 tsp. salt
1 tsp. nutmeg
2 1/2 tsp. cinnamon
1/2 tsp. ginger
1 tsp. baking soda
1 cup cooked pumpkin
1 cup raisins
1 cup chopped nuts

Directions:

1. Preheat oven to 375 degrees F.
2. Beat oil and eggs with rotary beater until well emulsified.
3. Add sugar substitute and beat until light and fluffy.
4. Add pumpkin, then dry ingredients.
5. Add raisins and nuts.
6. Drop by teaspoonful onto greased cookie sheet.
7. Bake for 15 to 20 minutes.
8. Cool on wire cookie racks.
9. Serve and enjoy!

Sugar Free Applesauce Cookies

Ingredients:

2 large eggs
2 tbsp. vegetable oil
1 cup unsweetened applesauce
2 tbsp. frozen concentrated apple juice, unsweetened
2 cups almond flour
1/2 tsp. baking powder
1 tsp. cinnamon
1/2 tsp. nutmeg
2 cups unsweetened granola (recipe below)

Granola Recipe:

1. Combine any of the following in equal amounts: rolled oats, chopped nuts, flaked coconut, finely chopped dried fruit, seeds.

Cookie Directions:

1. Preheat oven to 350 degrees F.
2. In a mixing bowl beat together eggs, oil, applesauce, and apple juice concentrate.
3. Add almond flour, baking powder, and spices.
4. Beat well and set aside.
5. In a small bowl, combine equal amounts of rolled oats, chopped nuts, flaked coconut, finely chopped dried fruit and seeds.
6. Mix in granola.
7. Drop batter by tsps. onto oiled baking sheets.
8. Bake for 10 minutes or until firm to the touch and bottoms are browned.
9. Cool on wire cookie racks.
10. Serve and enjoy!

Sugar Free Oatmeal Cookies

Ingredients:

3 tbsp. diet butter
2/3 cup non-fat dry milk
4 tbsp. raisins
1/2 tsp. baking soda
1 tsp. cinnamon
2 tbsp. vanilla
1 lg. mashed banana
1 tsp. baking powder
1/2 tsp. cream of tartar
1 1/2 tsp. brown sugar substitute
2 tbsp. lemon juice
1 1/2 cup quick rolled oats

Directions:

1. Preheat oven to 375 degrees F.
2. Mix all above ingredients.
3. Drop spoonfuls on to lightly greased cookie sheet.
4. Bake at for 10 to 12 minutes.
5. Cool on wire cookie racks.
6. Serve and enjoy!

Cream Cheese Cookies

Ingredients:

1 cup butter, softened
1 8 oz. pkg. cream cheese, softened
2 cups flour
1 cup Sugar substitute
1/4 tsp. salt
Dried fruit (apricots, dates, peaches, prunes, etc.)

Directions:

1. Preheat oven to 350 degrees F.
2. In a medium bowl, mix butter, cream cheese, flour and sugar substitute.
3. Refrigerate.
4. Roll out on a lightly floured work surface and cut into small circles.
5. Place one apricot half on top of circle of dough on top.
6. Seal around edges.
7. Bake for 10 minutes or until golden brown.
8. Cool on a wire cookie rack.
9. Serve and enjoy!

Chocolate Cookies

Ingredients:

1/4 cup canned evaporated milk
1/4 cup butter
1 tbsp. Sweet 10 liquid sweetener
1/2 tsp. vanilla
2 tbsp. unsweetened cocoa powder
1/2 cup bottled wheat germ
1/2 cup finely chopped walnuts or pecans

Directions:

1. In small saucepan, combine milk and butter, heating slowly until butter melts.
2. Stir in sweetener and vanilla.
3. Mix well.
4. Stir in cocoa powder until dissolved.
5. Remove from heat.
6. Add wheat germ and nuts.
7. Mix well.
8. Drop by the teaspoonful onto a tray lined with waxed-paper.
9. Cool on a wire cookie rack.
10. Serve and enjoy!

Peanut Butter Cookies

Ingredients:

1 cup and 2 tbsp. all-purpose flour
1/2 cup sugar substitute
1 1/2 tsp. baking powder
2/3 cup creamy peanut butter
1/4 cup cooking oil
1 egg
2 tbsp. water
1 tsp. vanilla

Directions:

1. Preheat oven to 375 degrees F.
2. Place flour, sugar substitute and baking powder in mixing bowl.
3. Add peanut butter, cooking oil, egg, water and vanilla.
4. Mix well.
5. Shape into 1 inch balls and place onto ungreased cookie sheets. Flatten with fork.
6. Bake 10 to 12 minutes or until lightly browned.
7. Cool on a wire cookie rack.
8. Serve and enjoy!

Lemon Cookies

Ingredients:

1 stick butter
1 tbsp. liquid sweetener or 12 saccharin tablets dissolved in 1 tsp. water
1 egg, beaten
1 tsp. vanilla
1 tsp. grated lemon peel
1 cup flour
1/2 tsp. baking soda
1/4 tsp. salt
Pecan halves for tops

Directions:

1. Preheat oven to 375 degrees F.
2. Cream butter.
3. Add sweetener; egg, vanilla, lemon and beat well.
4. Combine flour, soda, and salt.
5. Add to butter mixture and mix well.
6. Drop by tsps. onto ungreased cookie sheet.
7. Press flat with fork.
8. Press pecan half on top.
9. Bake in oven for 8-10 minutes.
10. Cool on a wire cookie rack.
11. Serve and enjoy!

original recipe stinks

Chocolate Chip Cookies

Ingredients:

~~1/2~~ cup butter, softened *2 sticks*
~~1~~ egg *2*
1/2 cup ~~sugar substitute~~ for baking *Monk Fruit*
~~1/2 cup milk~~ *brown Monk Fruit*
1 tsp. vanilla
~~1~~ cup flour *2 ¼ C*
1/2 tsp. baking soda
2 oz. dietetic chocolate bar cut into small chunks *1 12oz bag*

Directions: *½ t salt*

1. Preheat oven to ~~350~~ *375* degrees F.
2. Combine butter, egg, sugar substitute, vanilla, and milk.
3. Beat 1 minute at medium speed.
4. Add flour and baking soda.
5. Beat 2 minutes at low speed.
6. Fold in chocolate bar pieces.
7. Drop by the teaspoonful onto an ungreased cookie sheet.
8. Bake for 20-25 minutes until golden brown. *375° 8 mins*
9. Cool on a wire cookie rack.
10. Serve and enjoy!

No Sugar Sugar Cookies

Ingredients:

3/4 cup unsalted butter
1/4 cup light butter
1 cup granulated sugar substitute
1 tbsp. vanilla
1/4 cup egg substitute
1/4 cup water
3/4 tsp. cider vinegar
1 1/2 cups all-purpose flour
1 1/2 cups cake flour
1/4 tsp. salt
1 tsp. baking powder

Directions:

1. Preheat oven to 350 degrees F.
2. Lightly oil a cookie sheet and set aside.
3. Blend together butters, sugar substitute and vanilla in a medium mixing bowl with an electric mixer.
4. Blend until butter is softened.
5. Add egg substitute, water and vinegar.
6. Mix briefly.
7. Add flours, salt and baking powder.
8. Mix on low speed, until dough is formed.
9. Do not overmix.
10. Remove dough from bowl and place on a floured work surface.
11. Divide dough in half. Pat each half into a circle and cover with plastic wrap.
12. Refrigerate approximately 1 hour, allowing dough to chill.
13. Remove dough from refrigerator and roll out on a floured work surface to desired thickness, approx. 1/4 inch.
14. Cut with cookie cutters.
15. Place cookies on prepared sheet.
16. Bake for 10-12 minutes or until lightly browned on the back.
17. Cool on a wire cookie rack.
18. Serve and enjoy!

Raspberry Heart Cookies

Ingredients:

3/4 cup unsalted butter, room temperature
1/4 cup ~~light~~ butter, room temperature
1 cup granulated ~~sugar substitute~~ MonkFruit
1 tbsp. vanilla
1/4 cup egg ~~substitute~~
1/4 cup water
3/4 tsp. white vinegar
1 1/2 cups all-purpose flour
1 1/2 cups cake flour
1/4 tsp. salt
1 tsp. baking powder
1/3 cup low sugar or no sugar raspberry jam
3 oz. sugar free chocolate, melted

Directions:

1. Blend together butters, sugar substitute and vanilla in a medium mixing bowl.
2. Blend until butter is softened.
3. Add egg substitute, water and vinegar.
4. Mix briefly.
5. Add flours, salt and baking powder.
6. Mix with electric mixer on low speed until dough is formed, do not overmix.
7. Remove dough from bowl and place on a floured work surface.
8. Divide dough in half. Pat each half into a circle.
9. Cover with plastic wrap and refrigerate at least 1 hour.
10. Preheat oven to 350 degrees F.
11. Lightly oil a baking pan or cookie sheet. Set aside.
12. Remove dough from refrigerator and roll out on a floured work surface to approximately 1/8-inch thickness.
13. Cut with two-inch heart shaped cookie cutter.
14. Cut small heart shapes out of the center of half of the cookies (these will be the tops of the finished cookies).
15. Place cookies on prepared cookie sheet.
16. Bake for 8-10 minutes or until lightly browned on the bottom.
17. Cool on a wire cookie rack.
18. Spread 1 teasponn raspberry jam in the center of the larger heart cookies.
19. Flip over the smaller cutout hearts and drizzle melted chocolate on the underside.
20. Carefully place the smaller cutout hearts, chocolate side down, on top of the larger heart cookies so the raspberry jam shows through.

21. Push down lightly.
22. Serve and enjoy!

Snickerdoodles

Filling Ingredients:

2 oz. cream cheese, softened
2 tbsp. butter, softened
1 cup sugar substitute
1 large egg
1 tsp. vanilla extract
1 1/4 cups almond flour
1/2 tsp. baking soda
1/2 tsp. cinnamon
1/4 tsp. salt

Cinnamon Topping Ingredients:

2 tbsp. ~~sugar substitute~~ Monk Fruit
1 tsp. cinnamon

Directions:

1. Preheat oven to 375 degrees F.
2. Line a sheet pan with parchment paper.
3. Using a mixer, add the cream cheese, butter, sugar substitute, egg and vanilla extract to the mixing bowl, and beat on high until creamy and fluffy.
4. Add in Almond Flour, baking soda, cinnamon and salt, and mix on medium until well blended.
5. Using a tsp. or 1 oz. ice cream scoop, drop 16 evenly spaced cookies on the prepared sheet pan, and push down slightly on each.
6. Combine the cinnamon topping ingredients, and sprinkle evenly over the top of each cookie.
7. Bake for 8-10 minutes, or until they begin to brown around the edges.
8. Cool on a wire cookie rack.
9. Serve and enjoy!

Low Carb Almond Cookies

Ingredients:

cups almond flour
1/2 cup sugar substitute for baking
1/2 cup softened unsalted butter
1/2 tsp. salt
1 tsp. vanilla extract
1 tsp. almond extract
1 egg

Directions:

1. Preheat oven to 300 degrees F.
2. Blend softened butter for one minute with an electric mixer.
3. Add remaining ingredients and mix together.
4. Form dough into walnut sized balls and place onto ungreased cookie sheet.
5. Bake for 5 minutes.
6. Press down lightly with fork, then continue to bake another 18 minutes.
7. Cool on a wire cookie rack.
8. Serve and enjoy!

Thumbprint Cookies

1 cup sugar substitute
1 large egg
2 tbsp. milk
1 tsp. vanilla extract
1 1/4 cups almond flour
1/4 tsp. baking powder
/4 tsp. baking soda
•1/4 tsp. salt
3/4 cup sugar free jam of choice (strawberry, raspberry, grape, etc.)

Directions:

1. Preheat oven to 350 degrees F.
2. Beat butter sugar substitute.
3. Add egg, milk, & vanilla
4. Combine almond flour, baking powder, baking soda and salt
5. Shape dough by teaspoonful into balls.
6. Place on sprayed baking sheet
7. Press thumb into dough to form indentation
8. Bake in oven to 12 minutes
9. Fill each cookie with sugar free jam
10. Serve and enjoy!

Almond Crescent Cookies

Ingredients:

½ cup salted butter or margarine, softened
Pinch of kosher salt
¾ cup granulated sugar substitute
½ tsp vanilla extract
1 tsp almond extract
2 cups almond flour
1 cup sliced almonds

Directions:

1. Preheat oven to 350 degrees F.
2. Beat the butter, salt, and sweetener until fluffy.
3. Add the vanilla and almond extracts and blend well.
4. Add the almond flour and beat until just blended to a stiff dough.
5. Divide the dough in to about 12 balls.
6. Roll each ball into a 3 inch log.
7. Spread the sliced almonds onto a clean surface and crush slightly into smaller pieces with the heel of your hand.
8. Roll the logs in the almond pieces and then bend the two ends in and pinch slightly to create a crescent shape.
9. Place the almond crescents on a parchment lined cookie sheet and bake for 15 minutes.
10. Cool on a wire cookie rack.
11. Serve and enjoy!

Low Carb Thin Mint Macaroons

Ingredients:

2 cups unsweetened coconut
1/2 cup unsweetened almond milk
1 1/2 tsp peppermint extract
1/2 cup granulated sweetener
3 egg whites
1/4 tsp xanthan gum
1 oz. 90% or greater cacao dark chocolate

Directions:

1. Combine the coconut, almond milk, peppermint extract, and sweetener in a medium bowl and stir well.
2. In a separate large bowl whisk the egg whites and xanthan gum together until soft peaks form.
3. Fold the egg mixture into the coconut mixture until fully combined.
4. Drop the dough mixture by scoop or tbsp. into 24 mounds onto a parchment-lined cookie sheet.
5. Flatten into disks with your hand or a flat spatula.
6. Bake in a preheated 325 degree (F) oven for 16 minutes or until slightly firm.
7. Remove and cool.
8. Place the chocolate in a sealable bag and melt in the microwave for 30 seconds at a time until just liquid.
9. Snip a tiny corner off of the bag and squeeze the chocolate out onto the cookies in a circular pattern.
10. Cool on a wire cookie rack.
11. Serve and enjoy!

Low Carb Pinwheel Cookies

Filling Ingredients:

3 oz. cream cheese
1/4 cup sugar substitute
1 tsp. vanilla
3/4 cup coconut
3/4 cup pecans, finely chopped

Cookie dough Ingredients:

1/3 cup butter
3/4 cup sugar substitute
1/2 tsp. baking soda
Pinch of salt
1 egg
1 Tbsp. milk
3/4 cup cocoa powder
1 cup almond flour

Directions:

1. Lay out a piece of parchment paper and rolling pin.
2. Mix together all filling ingredients and set aside.
3. For cookie dough, cream together butter and sugar.
4. Add baking soda, salt, egg, and milk.
5. Mix in cocoa.
6. Mix in almond flour until just combined.
7. Dust parchment paper with extra cocoa powder.
8. Roll out half the dough, using more cocoa powder to keep dough from sticking to rolling pin to 8" x 10" rectangle.
9. Use an angled rubber spatula to spread half the filling carefully over the dough.
10. Starting on one of the long sides, carefully roll it up.
11. Cover with plastic wrap and refrigerate for at least a couple of hours.
12. Repeat with remaining dough and filling.
13. Remove from the refrigerator and cut into thin ¼ inch slices.
14. Preheat oven to 350° F.
15. Place cookies on a cookie sheet.
16. Bake for 9 minutes.
17. Cool on a wire cookie rack.
18. Serve and enjoy!

Low Carb Cocoa Cookies

Ingredients:

1 cup pecan halves
1/2 cup butter
1/4 cup sugar substitute
1/4 cup brown sugar substitute
1/3 cup cocoa powder
1 egg
3 Tbsp. milk
1/8 tsp. baking soda
Pinch of salt
1 tsp. vanilla
1 cup almond flour

Directions:

1. Preheat oven to 350 degrees F.
2. Set aside 38 nice looking pecan halves.
3. Chop the rest of the pecans.
4. Toast chopped pecans in the oven inside a pie pan for 7 minutes.
5. Let cool.
6. Cream together butter, brown sugar substitute, sugar substitute, and cocoa.
7. Add egg and milk.
8. Mix in salt, baking soda, and vanilla.
9. Add roasted pecans and almond flour.
10. Stir until mixed in.
11. Using a tsp., place dough on cookie sheets.
12. Place a pecan half on each cookie.
13. Bake for 9 minutes or until edges are crispy.
14. Cool on a wire cookie rack.
15. Serve and enjoy!

Pies

Sugar Free Lemon Cream Pie

Ingredients:

2 packages (4-serving-size) sugar-free lemon gelatin
2 cups boiling water
1 cup ice cubes
2 cups frozen sugar free whipped topping, thawed

Directions:

1. In a large bowl, dissolve gelatin in boiling water.
2. Add ice cubes and stir until melted.
3. Add sugar free whipped topping.
4. Fold together gently.
5. Pour into a 9-inch deep-dish pie plate.
6. The whipped topping will naturally separate from the gelatin once poured into the pie plate, creating a top layer.
7. Cover, and chill at least 3 hours, or until set.

Sugar Free Key Lime Pie

Ingredients:

1 (4-serving) package sugar-free lime gelatin
½ cup boiling water
1 (8-oz.) package fat-free cream cheese, softened
1 tbsp. fresh lime juice
1 tsp. grated lime peel
2 cups frozen light whipped topping, thawed

Directions:

1. Coat a 9-inch pie plate with cooking spray.
2. In a small bowl, dissolve gelatin in boiling water, stirring until dissolved.
3. In a large bowl, beat cream cheese until smooth.
4. Slowly add liquid gelatin until well combined.
5. Stir in lime juice and lime peel.
6. Fold in whipped topping until well blended.
7. Pour into pie plate, cover, and chill 3 hours or until set.

Sugar Free Banana Cream Pie

Ingredients:

1 cup skim milk
1 (4-serving) package sugar-free instant vanilla pudding mix
1 large ripe banana, peeled and sliced
1 (9") Diabetic Graham Cracker Pie Crust (see recipe below)
1 (8 oz.) container frozen sugar free whipped topping, thawed and divided
2 tbsps. toasted coconut (optional)

Directions:

1. In a large bowl, using a wire whisk, combine milk and pudding mix until thickened.
2. Make the pie crust.
3. Place banana slices on bottom of pie crust.
4. Fold half the whipped topping into the pudding.
5. Spoon pudding mixture evenly over bananas then spoon remaining whipped topping over pudding mixture and sprinkle with toasted coconut, if desired.
6. Cover and chill at least 4 hours, or until ready to serve.

Sugar Free Apple Pie

Ingredients:

6 cups sliced and pared tart apples
4 (1 g) packets artificial sweetener
1 tbsp. cornstarch
1/2 tsp. cinnamon
2 tbsps. low fat margarine
2 low carb pie crusts (see recipe below)

Directions:

1. Mix sweetener, cornstarch, and cinnamon.
2. Pour over apples and mix well.
3. Pour apple mixture into bottom unbaked pie crust.
4. Cut oleo into small pieces and put on top of apples.
5. Cover with remaining second crust and seal edges.
6. Bake at 425 degrees for 15 minutes.
7. Lower temperature to 350 degrees and continue baking for an additional 30-40 minutes.

Low Sugar Pumpkin Pie

Ingredients:

9" unbaked pie shells
2/3 cup brown sugar substitute
1/2 tsp. salt
1 1/2 tsps. cinnamon
1/4 tsp. nutmeg
1/8 tsp. clove
1/8 tsp. ginger
2 cups pumpkin
3 eggs, beaten
3/4 cup evaporated milk
1/4 cup milk

Directions:

1. Preheat oven to 425 degrees.
2. Combine sweetener, salt and spices.
3. Blend in pumpkin, eggs and milks.
4. Pour into pastry shell.
5. Bake 425 for 15mins
6. Reduce heat to 400 and bake until knife inserted comes out clean

Low Carb Pecan Pie

Ingredients:

2 tbsps. artificial sweetener
1 tbsp. coconut flour
1/3 cup brown sugar substitute
1/4 cup butter substitute
2 Eggs 1 tbsp. fat free milk
1 tsp. vanilla extract
1 cup chopped pecans

Directions:

1. Pre-heat oven to 350 degrees.
2. In a large mixing bowl, mix the eggs and butter.
3. Combine and mix flour, brown sugar substitute and artificial sweetener.
4. Mix in the milk, pecans and vanilla extract.
5. Pour mixture into a 9 inch shortbread pie pan.
6. Bake for 35 to 40 minutes.

Low Carb Chicken Pot Pie

Ingredients:

1 pound boneless skinless chicken breasts
1 cup carrots, sliced
1/2 cup mushrooms, sliced
1 onion, chopped
1/2 cup sweet potatoes, peeled and diced
1 tsp. thyme leaves
4 tbsps. all-purpose flour
2 cup fat-free low-sodium chicken broth
1/2 cup peas
2 low carb pie crusts (recipe below) – one batch for the bottom and one for the top
Salt
Pepper

Directions:

1. Preheat your oven to 400 degrees.
2. In a skillet coated with cooking spray, cook the chicken breasts over medium heat for 7-10 minutes.
3. Season with salt and pepper and cut into pieces.
4. Recoat the skillet with cooking spray.
5. Sauté the carrots, mushrooms, onion, and potatoes until tender.
6. Add the thyme and flour, stirring for 30 seconds.
7. Gradually add the chicken broth, stirring over medium heat until thickened.
8. Add the chicken and peas and cook another 5 minutes.
9. Coat a 9-inch pie plate with cooking spray.
10. Lay the bottom pie crust in the pan.
11. Fill with the chicken mixture.
12. Lay the second pie crust on top and cut slits to vent.
13. Bake for 10-12 minutes or until golden brown.

Low Carb Shepherds Pie

Ingredients:

16 oz. of ground beef
5-7 baby portabella mushrooms chopped
½ medium sized red bell pepper chopped
¼ cup of dice red onions
16 oz. bag of frozen cauliflower
¼ cup chicken broth
3 tsp garlic minced
1 tsp fresh rosemary
1 tsp fresh thyme
1 tsp cumin
¾ cup beef broth
⅛-1/2 tsp of Xanthan gum
Salt and pepper

Directions:

1. Preheat oven to 350 degrees.
2. Brown ground beef on medium setting until cooked through.
3. While ground beef is browning, chop all vegetables.
4. Heat up bag of frozen cauliflower in microwave until steaming and cooked through.
5. Add to blender and add chicken broth and 1 tsp. garlic.
6. Blend until smooth.
7. Transfer ground beef to side dish
8. Add vegetables, herbs, and ½ of beef broth to the same pan.
9. Sauté vegetables.
10. Add back ground beef and remaining beef broth to the pan of sautéed vegetables and stir.
11. Add a small amount of Xanthan gum at a time and mix throughout to thicken the beef broth like a gravy.
12. Transfer meat and vegetable mix to a baking dish and.
13. Spread on mashed cauliflower until evenly coated.
14. Place in the oven for 20-30 minutes until bubbly on the sides.
15. Remove from the oven and let it rest for about 5 minutes before serving

Sugar Free Chocolate Pie

Ingredients:

2 tbsps. flour
1/4 cup granulated sugar substitute
3 tbsps. cocoa powder
2 tbsps. butter, melted
2 eggs
1 cup buttermilk
1 tsp. vanilla extract
1 9"sugar free unbaked pie shell

Directions:

1. In a mixing bowl, stir flour, sugar substitute and cocoa until well blended.
2. With an electric mixer on low speed, beat in the melted butter.
3. Beat in eggs until thoroughly blended.
4. Beat in buttermilk and vanilla.
5. Pour mixture into pie shell.
6. Bake at 350 degrees F for 1 hour or until filling is set.

Cherry Pie

Ingredients:

2 low carb pie crusts (see recipe below) one for the bottom and one for the top
2 (14.5 oz.) cans pitted tart red cherries, undrained
2/3 cup granulated sugar substitute
1/4 cup cornstarch
2 tsps. fresh lemon juice
1/4 tsp. almond extract
4 drops red food coloring

Directions:

1. Preheat oven to 375 degrees F.
2. Make pie crusts.
3. Spray pie pan with cooking spray.
4. Fit pie crust into a 9-inch pie plate.
5. Drain cherries, reserving 1 cup juice; set fruit aside.
6. Combine sweetener and cornstarch in a medium saucepan.
7. Gradually stir reserved juice into sweetener mixture.
8. Cook over medium heat, stirring constantly, until mixture begins to boil.
9. Boil for 1 minute, stirring constantly.
10. Remove from heat; stir in lemon juice, almond extract and food coloring, if desired.
11. Fold in reserved cherries; cool slightly.
12. Spoon mixture into bottom crust.
13. Place second pie crust over filling; fold edges under and crimp.
14. Cut slits in top to allow steam to escape.
15. Bake 40 to 50 minutes or until crust is golden.
16. Cover edges with aluminum foil to prevent over browning, if necessary.
17. Cool on a wire rack one hour before serving.

Low Sugar Peanut Butter Pie

Ingredients:

1 graham cracker pie crust (see recipe below)
8 oz. cream cheese
1/2 cup peanut butter
1 cup artificial sweetener
12 oz. sugar free non-dairy whipped topping

Directions:

1. Cream together cream cheese and sweetener.
2. Add peanut butter, cream well.
3. Stir in 2/3 of whipped topping.
4. Put into pie shell.
5. Top with remaining whipped topping.

Raspberry-Rhubarb Pie

Ingredients:

1 low carb pie crust (recipe below)
4 cups cut rhubarb
2/3 cup water
2 (4-serving) packages sugar-free raspberry gelatin
1 ½ cup frozen unsweetened raspberries
¼ cup granulated sugar substitute
1 cup fat-free frozen whipped topping, thawed

Directions:

1. Preheat oven to 450 degrees F.
2. Spray a pie plate with cooking spray.
3. Make pie crust.
4. Press in to pie plate.
5. Bake 9 to 11 minutes or until lightly browned.
6. Cool completely.
7. In a medium saucepan, combine rhubarb and water.
8. Cover and cook over medium heat until rhubarb is tender, about 10 minutes.
9. Remove from heat.
10. Add dry gelatin; mix well to dissolve gelatin.
11. Stir in frozen raspberries.
12. Cool completely.
13. Fold in granulated sugar substitute and whipped topping.
14. Mix gently to combine.
15. Pour into cooled pie crust.
16. Refrigerate 2 hours or until ready to serve.

Low Sugar Strawberry Pie

Ingredients:

4 cups sliced strawberries (no sugar added if frozen)
1 box fat free and sugar free cooked vanilla pudding
2 cups cold water
1 box sugar free strawberry gelatin
Sugar free whipped topping

Directions:

1. Place sliced strawberries in pie plate.
2. Cook pudding as directed, substituting water for milk.
3. When pudding comes to full boil remove from heat.
4. Stir in gelatin.
5. Cool slightly and pour over strawberries.
6. Chill until set.
7. Top with sugar free whipped topping if desired.

Low Sugar Sweet Potato Pie

Ingredients:

1 pound sweet potatoes
1/2 cup margarine, softened
1 cup granular sugar substitute
1/2 cup low-fat milk
2 eggs
1/2 tsp. ground nutmeg
1/2 tsp. ground cinnamon
1 tsp. vanilla extract
1/2 tsp. lemon extract
1 (9 inch) unbaked sugar free pie shell

Directions:

1. Boil sweet potatoes whole in skin for 40 to 50 minutes, or until done.
2. Run cold water over the sweet potato, and remove the skin.
3. Break apart sweet potato in a bowl.
4. Add margarine, and mix well with mixer.
5. Stir in sugar substitute, milk, eggs, nutmeg, cinnamon and vanilla.
6. Beat on medium speed until mixture is smooth.
7. Pour filling into an unbaked pie crust.
8. Bake at 350 degrees F (175 degrees C) for 55 to 60 minutes, or until knife inserted in center comes out clean.
9. Pie will puff up like a soufflé, and then will sink down as it cools.

Low Sugar Peach Pie

Ingredients:

2 low carb pie crusts (recipe below) – one for the bottom and one for the top
2 tbsps. lemon juice
1 1/4 cup sugar substitute
1/8 tsp Salt
1/4 tsp nutmeg
4 tbsp. butter
1 1/2 pound fresh peaches (6 c sliced)
2 tbsp. sugar substitute
1/4 tsp cinnamon
3 tbsp. flour
1 cup sugar free whipped topping

Directions:

1. Make pie crusts.
2. Set aside.
3. Sprinkle lemon juice over peach slices in large bowl.
4. Mix 1 1/4 cup sugar substitute with the salt, nutmeg, cinnamon and flour.
5. Add to peaches.
6. Toss until evenly coated.
7. Spray a pie pan with cooking spray.
8. Press first crust in to pie pan.
9. Add peach mixture.
10. Lay second pie crust on top.
11. Flute edges and cut slits to vent.
12. Bake 10 minutes at 450 degrees, then reduce heat to 350 degrees and bake 30 minutes more.
13. Serve with sugar free whipped topping.

Low Sugar Blueberry Pie

Ingredients:

4 cup blueberries, fresh or thawed frozen (unsweetened)
4 tsps. sugar substitute
1/4 tsps. cinnamon
1/8 tsps. nutmeg
1 tbsps. lemon juice
2 tbsps. quick tapioca
8-10 drops liquid butter flavoring
2 low carb pie crust (recipe below) – one batch for the bottom and one for the top

Directions:

1. Line 10" pie plate with bottom crust
2. Wash and drain berries.
3. Mix next 6 ingredients together in small bowl
4. Toss with berries being careful to not crush the berries too much.
5. Pour berries in to the crust.
6. Cover with top crust, slit for steam to escape.
7. Bake at 425 for 10 minutes, reduce heat to 325 for 45 minutes or until crust is golden brown and filling is bubbly.
8. Cool on wire rack, serve with dollop of sugar free whipped topping.

Low Sugar Berry Pie

Ingredients:

2 cups plain fat-free Greek yogurt
2 tbsps. sugar free powdered sugar (see recipe below)
1/2 tsp. vanilla
Non-stick cooking spray
1 1/3 cups finely crushed zwieback crackers (about 17 slices)
2 tbsps. packed sugar free brown sugar
1 egg white, lightly beaten
2 tbsps. butter, melted
3/4 cup low-calorie cranberry-raspberry drink
1 tbsp. corn starch
6 cups fresh raspberries, blackberries, blueberries, and/or halved strawberries
1 1/2 cups frozen sugar free whipped dessert topping, thawed
3/4 tsp. finely shredded lemon peel

Directions:

1. In a small bowl, combine yogurt, powdered sugar, and vanilla.
2. Cover and chill until ready to use.
3. Preheat oven to 350 degrees F.
4. Coat a 9-inch pie plate with non-stick cooking spray.
5. In a medium bowl, combine finely crushed zwieback crackers and brown sugar.
6. Add egg white and melted butter; stir until well mixed.
7. Press mixture evenly onto bottom and up side of prepared pie plate.
8. Bake for 10 to 12 minutes or until edge is browned.
9. Cool completely on a wire rack.
10. In a small saucepan, stir together cranberry-raspberry drink and corn starch.
11. Cook and stir over medium heat until thickened and bubbly.
12. Cook and stir for 2 minutes more the remove from heat.
13. Transfer to a small bowl.
14. Cover surface with plastic wrap.
15. Let stand at room temperature for 1 to 2 hours or until cooled.
16. Spread yogurt mixture into crust-lined pie plate.
17. In a large bowl, gently toss berries and cooled glaze.
18. Spoon over yogurt mixture.
19. Cover and chill before serving.

Diabetic Graham Cracker Pie Crust

Ingredients:

1 cup graham crackers, finely crushed
1/2 cup butter or margarine, melted

Directions:

1. Preheat oven to 350 degrees F.
2. Combine the crushed graham cracker crumbs and melted margarine or butter in a bowl.
3. Mix well.
4. Press in to a pie pan.

Sugar Free Powdered Sugar

Ingredients:

1 cup xylitol
1-2 tsp arrowroot or cornstarch, to prevent clumping when stored (optional)

Directions:

1. Put ingredients in a blender.
2. Blend until a fine powder.

Low Carb Pie Crust

Ingredients:

1/2 cup butter
2 whole Eggs
1/4 tsp. Sea Salt
3/4 cup Coconut Flour
 Stevia or sugar substitute (to taste)

Directions:

1. Preheat oven to 400 degrees.
2. In medium bowl, beat butter, eggs, and salt together with a fork.
3. Add coconut flour.
4. Mix well, until there are no clumps.
5. Gather dough into a ball, then pat it into a 9-inch greased pie pan.
6. Prick dough with a fork several times.
7. Bake for 9 minutes, then let cool.
8. If baking a top crust, roll the dough out instead of patting into the pie pan.

Cakes

Low Carb Berry Sponge Cake

Ingredients:

4 oz. butter or margarine melted
½ cup coconut flour
3 -5 tbsp. granulated stevia, or sweetener of choice, to taste
2 tsp. vanilla
1 tsp. baking powder
8 eggs
1 cup frozen berries

Directions:

1. Preheat oven to 350 degrees F.
2. Mix the melted butter, coconut flour, stevia, vanilla and baking powder together until smooth.
3. Add the eggs one by one, mixing in between each addition.
4. Pour into a prepared baking dish, I use a silicon cake dish.
5. Press each frozen berry evenly into the cake. This allows the berries to be evenly distributed and not clump together. It also stops the cake from turning pink!
6. Bake for 20-25 minutes until cooked in the center.
7. Serve with yogurt and berries.

Sugar Free Lemon Cheesecake

Ingredients:

1 (3 oz.) package sugar-free lemon gelatin
2 tbsps. lemon juice
2 (8 oz.) packages cream cheese
1 cup boiling water

Directions:

1. Stir the boiling water into the box of gelatin, mixing for about two minutes.
2. Add the cream cheese and lemon juice.
3. Mix until all lumps have disappeared.
4. Pour into an 8" square pan and chill until set.
5. Cut into 8 squares.

Low Carb Lemon Coconut Cake

Ingredients:

3.5 oz. ground almonds
3.5 oz. desiccated/shredded coconut
2 tsp. baking powder
2 tbs. granulated stevia
1 tsp. psyllium husk
1.8 oz. melted butter or coconut oil
3 eggs
Zest and juice of 2 lemons

Icing Ingredients:

3.5 oz. cream cheese softened
3.5 oz. natural yoghurt
Zest of 1 lemon
1 tbsp. granulated stevia, or to taste

Cake Directions:

1. Preheat oven to 350 degrees F.
2. Mix ground almonds, coconut, baking powder, stevia and psyllium husk together.
3. Add the melted butter into the center and mix gently.
4. Add the eggs, mix.
5. Add the lemon juice and zest.
6. Mix, then pour into a greased and lined ring tin.
7. Bake for 25-30 minutes.

Icing Directions:

1. Mix the softened cream cheese with the yogurt.
2. Add the stevia and lemon zest.
3. Mix well.
4. Carefully ice the cake.

Low Carb Carrot Cake

Ingredients:

5 eggs
7 oz. butter melted
3 tbsp. granulated stevia
2 tsp vanilla
3 cups grated/shredded carrots
½ cup chopped walnuts
½ cup shredded unsweetened coconut
1 ½ cups ground almonds or almond flour
1 tsp. ground cinnamon
1 tsp. mixed spice
2 tsp. baking powder

Icing Ingredients:

1 cup cream cheese
1 tbsp. granulated stevia

Cake Directions:

1. Preheat oven to 350 degrees F.
2. Beat eggs, melted butter, stevia, and vanilla together.
3. Add grated carrot, walnuts, and coconut then mix ground almonds, spices and baking powder.
4. Pour into a greased and lined tin.
5. Bake for 30 minutes or until a toothpick inserted in the center comes out clean.

Icing Directions:

1. Warm the cream cheese in the microwave for 20 seconds to soften it.
2. Stir in 1 tbsp. stevia.
3. Cover with cream cheese frosting.

Low Carb Key Lime Cheesecake

Ingredients:

1 tbsp. wheat germ
2 cups plus 1 tbsp. sugar substitute
16 oz. real cream cheese, room temperature
1 cup sour cream
1 cup whole milk ricotta cheese
3/4 cup Key lime juice
2 tbsps. no sugar added vanilla extract
1/4 cup hot water
2 limes, zested, divided
3 envelopes unflavored gelatin
3/4 cup boiling water

Directions:

1. Sprinkle the wheat germ and 1 tbsp. sugar substitute over the bottom of a pie pan to create a crust.
2. In the bowl of an electric mixer, beat the softened cream cheese, sour cream, ricotta cheese, lime juice, 2 cups sugar substitute, vanilla extract, 1/4 cup hot water, and zest of 1 lime on medium speed until well combined.
3. Using a fork to mix, thoroughly dissolve the 3 envelopes of gelatin in 3/4 cup boiling water.
4. Do not let cool and move onto the next step immediately.
5. (You must the water be boiling hot and that you mix the gelatin powder in quickly so it is completely dissolved.)
6. With the mixer on high, work quickly so the gelatin does not set.
7. Blend the hot dissolved gelatin thoroughly into cheesecake mixture.
8. Immediately pour mixture into the prepared pie pan and sprinkle with the zest of the other lime.
9. Chill in the refrigerator for about 3 to 4 hours or until firm.
10. Serve and enjoy!
11. Put any leftover in the freezer for 5-10 minutes to firm to whipped cream consistency.
12. Use the leftover mixture to decorate the top by putting it in a plastic bag and snipping the end then squeezing it out along the edge.

Sugar-Free Chocolate Angel Food Cake

Ingredients:

1 cup cake flour
1 pkg. sugar substitute
3 tbsp. unsweetened cocoa
10 egg whites
1 1/2 tsp. cream of tartar
1 1/2 tsp. vanilla
¼ tsp. salt
3 pkgs. sugar substitute

Directions:

1. Preheat oven to 350 degrees F.
2. Sift together flour, 1 package sugar substitute, and 3 tbsps. of cocoa into a bowl.
3. Repeat sifting.
4. Set aside.
5. In a large bowl beat egg whites with cream of tartar, vanilla, and salt at medium speed till soft peaks form.
6. Gradually add 3 packages of sugar substitute, beating at high speed until stiff peaks form.
7. Fold in remaining ingredients.
8. Scoop into oiled and floured bundt pan,
9. Bake for 25 minutes.
10. Let cool.
11. Serve and enjoy!

Low Sugar Chocolate Layer Cake

Cake Ingredients:

2 cups almond flour
2/3 cup cocoa powder
1/3 cup coconut flour
1/3 cup unflavored whey protein powder
1 tbsp. baking powder
1 tbsp. instant coffee
½ tsp salt
½ cup butter, softened
1 cup granulated Swerve
4 eggs
1 tsp. vanilla extract
1 cup unsweetened almond milk

Frosting Ingredients:

7 oz. good quality unsweetened chocolate, chopped
1¾ cups whipping cream
¾ cup confectioner's Swerve Sweetener
½ tsp vanilla extract

Directions:

1. Preheat oven to 325 degrees F.
2. Grease three 9-inch circular cake pans.
3. Line with parchment circles and grease the parchment.
4. In a medium bowl, whisk together the almond flour, cocoa powder, coconut flour, whey protein powder, baking powder, coffee and salt.
5. In a large bowl, beat butter with Swerve until light and fluffy.
6. Beat in eggs and vanilla extract, then beat in half of the almond flour mixture.
7. Beat in nut milk and then the remaining almond flour mixture until well combined. Divide the batter evenly among the cake pans and smooth the tops with a knife or offset spatula.
8. Bake about 20 minutes, until the center is firm to the touch.
9. Remove and let cool in pans 15 minutes, then flip out onto a wire rack to cool completely.
10. To make the frosting, place chopped chocolate in a large bowl (in the bowl of a stand mixer, if you will be using one).
11. In a medium saucepan over medium heat, combine whipping cream and confectioner's Swerve.
12. Whisk until Swerve is dissolved.
13. Bring to just a simmer.
14. Pour over chopped chocolate and let sit about 10 minutes, until chocolate is melted. Whisk to combine.

15. Let cool to room temperature, about two hours.
16. Using whisk attachment of stand mixer or beater of hand-held mixer: beat on medium-high for 3 to 5 minutes, until lighter in color and fluffy.
17. Assemble cake by placing one layer of cake on a serving platter or cake stand and spread with about 1/3 of the whipped frosting.
18. Top with another cake layer and another 1/3 of frosting,
19. Top the final layer and remaining frosting.
20. Use a spatula to swirl frosting on the top.
21. Let set for at least 30 minutes before serving.

Chocolate Eclaire Cake

Pastry Cream Ingredients:

1 ¼ cups whipping cream
3 egg yolks
¼ cup Swerve Sweetener
pinch salt
1 tbsp. arrowroot starch
2 tbsp. butter, cut into two pieces
1 ½ tsp. vanilla extract
¼ tsp. stevia extract

Meringue Layers Ingredients:

3/4 cup fine almond flour
1/3 cup powdered Swerve Sweetener
4 egg whites, room temperature
2 tbsp. granulated Swerve Sweetener
½ tsp. vanilla extract
¼ tsp. cream of tartar
pinch salt

Chocolate Ganache Ingredients:

5 tbsp. butter
2 oz. unsweetened chocolate
¼ cup powdered Swerve Sweetener
1/2 tsp. vanilla extract

Pastry Cream Directions:

1. Bring whipping cream to a simmer in a medium saucepan over medium heat.
2. In a medium bowl, whisk egg yolks with sweetener and salt, then whisk in arrowroot starch* until mixture becomes pale yellow and thick, about 30 seconds.
3. Slowly whisk about half of the hot cream into the yolks to temper, then return the yolk/cream mixture back to the saucepan and cook until thick and glossy, about 1½ minutes, whisking continuously. It thickens up suddenly and quickly, so watch carefully!
4. Remove from heat and whisk in butter, vanilla and stevia.
5. Transfer to a small bowl and press plastic wrap flush to the surface.
6. Chill in refrigerator at least 3 hours.

Meringue Layers Directions:

1. Preheat oven to 350 degrees F.
2. On a large piece of parchment, trace three 5x10 inch rectangles.

3. Place parchment on a large baking sheet.
4. In a medium bowl, whisk together almond flour and powdered sweetener.
5. In a large, clean bowl, beat egg whites with granulated sweetener, vanilla extract, cream of tartar and salt until they just begin to hold stiff peaks.
6. Gently fold in almond flour mixture until fully combined.
7. Spread meringue mixture evenly onto each of the 3 traced rectangles.
8. Bake 15 minutes, then turn off oven and prop open door with a wooden spoon. Leave inside until cool.

Chocolate Ganache Directions:

1. In a medium saucepan over low heat, melt butter and unsweetened chocolate together, stirring until smooth.
2. Stir in powdered sweetener and vanilla extract.
3. Let cool 5 to 10 minutes, until thickened but still pourable.

Assembly Directions:

1. Peel one meringue layer carefully off parchment and lay on serving platter.
2. Spread with half of the pastry cream.
3. Top with another layer of meringue and spread with remaining half of pastry cream.
4. Top with final layer of meringue.
5. Pour ganache over top of cake and let drip down the sides.
6. Let set at least one hour before serving.

Strawberry Shortcake

Cake Ingredients:

8 eggs, separated
8 oz. cream cheese
1 tsp vanilla extract
1/8 tsp cream of tartar
1/2 cup sugar substitute equivalent
1 scoop protein powder
2 cups Fresh Strawberries, sliced plus sweetener (see directions below)
Whipped Topping (see recipe below)

Cake Directions:

1. Whip the whites with cream of tartar until stiff peaks form, about 5 minutes.
2. In a separate bowl, combine cream cheese with egg yolks, vanilla extract, protein powder, sweetener and salt.
3. Gently fold the whites into the yolk mixture until combined.
4. Spread the batter evenly on the sheet cake covered with parchment paper and bake in a 300 degree oven for 30 minutes.
5. Let cool 15 minutes with a damp dish towel on top to keep cake from drying out.
6. Cut cake into eight equal sections.
7. Set aside.

Strawberries Directions:

1. Soak in just enough water to almost cover the strawberries plus 1/4 cup equivalent sugar substitute.
2. Let sit for an hour or overnight in the refrigerator.

Cake Assembly Directions:

1. Place first cake layer on a plate.
2. Top with whipped cream (recipe below).
3. Top with second cake, whipped cream and strawberries.
4. Serve cold.

Whipped Cream Ingredients:

1 cup heavy whipping cream
4 tbsp. sugar substitute
1 tsp. vanilla extract

Whipped Cream Directions:

1. Whip all ingredients together.
2. Mix on high speed in a mixer until stiff peaks form.

Caramel Cupcakes

Cake Ingredients:

2 cups almond flour
1/4 cup unflavored whey protein powder (or powdered egg whites)
2 tsp baking powder
1/4 tsp salt
1 recipe sugar-free caramel sauce
2 large eggs
1 tsp caramel or vanilla extract
1/4 tsp liquid stevia extract
1/3 cup almond milk or cashew milk

Frosting Ingredients:

3 oz. (1 bar) Diabetic Creamy milk chocolate (such as Lily's)
1/2 cup butter, softened
2 cups powdered Swerve Sweetener
4 to 6 tbsp heavy whipping cream, room temperature
1/2 tsp vanilla extract

Cupcakes Directions:

1. Preheat oven to 325 degrees F.
2. Line a 12 cavity muffin tin with paper liners.
3. In a large bowl, whisk together almond flour, whey protein, baking powder, and salt.
4. Add caramel sauce, eggs, caramel or vanilla extract and nut milk until well combined.
5. Divide batter among prepared muffin tin and bake 28 to 30 minutes, or until a tester inserted in the center comes out clean.
6. Remove and let cool completely in pan.

Frosting Directions:

1. In a heatproof bowl set over a pan of barely simmering water.
2. Melt chocolate until smooth.
3. In a large bowl, beat butter with sweetener until combined and mixture resembles crumbs.
4. Add chocolate and beat until combined.
5. Add 4 tbsp. whipping cream and vanilla extract and beat until smooth.
6. If frosting is too thick, add additional whipping cream until a spreadable consistency is achieved.
7. Spread or pipe onto cooled cupcakes.

Coffee Crumb Cake

Cake Ingredients:

6 eggs, separated
6 oz. cream cheese, softened
1/2 cup sugar equivalent substitute
1/4 cup protein powder
1 tsp. vanilla extract
1/4 tsp. cream of tartar
1 tsp. cinnamon

Crumb topping Ingredients:

1 1/2 cups finely ground almond flour
2 tsp. cinnamon
1/2 cup brown sugar substitute
1/4 cup cold butter, cubed

Glaze Ingredients:

1/2 cup heavy whipping cream
1 Tbsp sugar equivalent substitute
1 tsp cinnamon
2 tsp softened butter

Cake Directions:

1. Preheat oven to 300 degrees F.
2. Separate the egg yolks from the whites.
3. Whip the whites with the cream of tartar until stiff peaks form.
4. Beat the egg yolks with cream cheese, sugar substitute, protein powder, vanilla extract, and cinnamon.
5. Fold this mixture with the eggs whites gently as not to deflate the whites.
6. Spoon mixture in an 8 inch square baking dish lined with parchment paper. You can also use an 8 inch spring form pan, generously greased with butter. Set aside.
7. Place almond flour, brown sugar substitute, cinnamon and butter in a bowl and combine with a fork until well combined.
8. Add half of the crumb topping to the cake batter evenly.
9. About half way through baking the cake, remove cake and add the remaining topping.
10. Continue baking.
11. Bake for 40-50 minutes, but be sure to start testing the batter after 30 minutes with a toothpick.

Glaze Directions:

1. Combine heavy cream, sweetener and cinnamon in a heat-proof measuring cup.
2. Heat in microwave or small sauce pan until sweetener has dissolved.
3. Mix well, adding butter and mix again. You can whip this to make it thicker when it's well chilled.
4. Drizzle glaze on semi cooled crumb cake.
5. Chill cake for 24 hours.
6. Serve and enjoy!

Boston Cream Napoleon

Ingredients:

3 eggs
3 oz. cream cheese
2 packets Splenda
1/8 tsp cream of tartar
pinch of salt
1 small Sugar free instant French Vanilla Pudding (Great Value)
1 & 1/2 cups of 1% Milk
1/3 Cup Heavy Whipping Cream
2 Tbsps. Sugar Free Chocolate Syrup (Great Value)

Directions:

1. Preheat oven to 300 degrees F.
2. With a mixer on high speed, mix whites with cream of tartar until stiff peaks form.
3. In a separate bowl, mix yolks with the Splenda, cream cheese, and added salt.
4. Combine yolk mixture by barely folding it in with the whites.
5. Bake in a medium-sized jelly roll pan on a silpat sprayed with cooking spray for 27 minutes.
6. Let cool.
7. Cut into 4 equal strips.
8. Mix pudding with milk, and layer like a lasagna.
9. Mix whipping cream with 1 tbsp. of chocolate syrup and whip until frosting-like in thickness.
10. Drizzle the top with the rest of the syrup.
11. Chill for 4 hours.
12. Serve and enjoy!

Tiramisu

Cake Ingredients:

Unsalted butter
1/2 cup almond flour
1/2 tsp. baking powder
1/8 tsp. salt
3 large eggs
2 tbsps. powdered erythritol
1/8 tsp. stevia extract powder
1/4 tsp. sugar free vanilla extract
1/4 tsp. almond extract
1/8 tsp. cream of tartar

Custard Ingredients:

6 egg yolks
2 tbsp. powdered erythritol
1-2 drops stevia glycerite
8 oz. mascarpone cheese
1 3/4 cups heavy or whipping cream
1/4 cup strong coffee or espresso
1-2 tbsp. rum or brandy

Cake Directions:

1. Grease a 11×7 inch pan with butter.
2. Line with parchment paper and grease with butter again.
3. Preheat the oven to 350 degrees F.
4. Combine the almond flour, baking powder and salt.
5. Separate the eggs.
6. With an electric mixer, beat the yolks and stevia until thick and lemon colored.
7. Beat in the vanilla, almond extract and cream of tartar.
8. Fold in the almond flour.
9. With a clean bowl and beaters, beat the egg whites to firm peaks.
10. Stir 1/4 into the almond mixture.
11. Fold in 1/2 of the remaining whites until barely combined and then the remaining 1/2 until thoroughly combined.
12. Spread evenly into the prepared pan.
13. Bake for 15-20 minutes until the top springs back when pressed lightly.
14. Let cool.

Custard Directions:

1. In small mixing bowl, beat egg yolks, erythritol and stevia until thick and lemon colored.
2. Place mixture in top of a double boiler over boiling water.

3. Reduce heat to low.
4. Cook 8-10 minutes, stirring constantly.
5. Remove from heat.
6. Add mascarpone cheese, beating well.
7. In a small mixing bowl, beat heavy or whipping cream until stiff peaks form. Fold into egg yolk mixture; set aside.

Assembly Directions:

1. Cut the almond cake into 16 fingers.
2. 1Combine the rum and espresso in a small bowl.
3. Sprinkle the bottom of a 9×5 bread pan lightly with cocoa then line with half the almond cake fingers.
4. Using a brush, lightly coat the cake fingers with the espresso mix being careful not to get them too wet.
5. Spread on 1/2 of the mascarpone mixture and dust the top with cocoa.
6. Repeat the layers.
7. End with a sprinkling of cocoa.
8. Cover and refrigerate overnight.

Pineapple Upside Down Cake

Ingredients:

1/4 cup butter, softened.
1/4 cup butter or spectrum palm oil.
1/4 cup coconut palm sugar (low carb brown sugar for the topping)
1/2 cup heavy cream
5 large eggs
1 tsp. vanilla extract
2 cups almond flour
1 or 2 packets stevia
1/2 cup of pineapple juice
1 can of pineapple slices (about 11 or 12)
12 Dark Mordello Cherries.

Directions:

1. Preheat oven to 350 degrees F.
2. Put 1/4 cup of butter in a rectangular baking dish and melt it in the oven.
3. Mix heavy cream, 1/4 cup butter, eggs, vanilla, stevia, and almond flour in an electric mixer.
4. Beat on high until the batter looks fluffy and whipped.
5. Slowly add the pineapple juice.
6. When the batter is ready, take out the pan with the melted butter.
7. Spread it around the pan evenly.
8. Sprinkle 1/4 cup of the coconut palm sugar evenly over the bottom of the baking dish.
9. Layer your 9-12 pineapple slices.
10. In the center of each pineapple slice place a cherry.
11. Pour the batter on top to barely cover the pinapple and cherries.
12. Bake 35-45 minutes, watched carefully so that it browns nicely.
13. Just watch it carefully to see how it is browning. When it is nice and brown it's ready to come out of the oven.
14. Flip upside down on to a platter.
15. Serve and enjoy!

Chocolate Pudding Cake

Ingredients:

2 cups unsalted butter
13 tbsps. Xylitol
2 tsps. vanilla extract
3 tsps. coconut extract
6 eggs
3/4 cups coconut flour
1 tsp. baking powder
1 tsp. salt
1 cup. coconut milk unsweetened
1 cup. dried coconut
16 oz. cream cheese

Directions:

1. Preheat oven to 325 degrees F.
2. Prepare two 9-inch round pans with cooking spray.
3. Cut out parchment paper to fit into the bottom of each pan and place the paper in the pan.
4. Spray parchment with cooking spray.
5. Set aside.
6. With an electric mixer beat 1 cup butter and then the 8 tbsps. of xylitol that was powdered until light and fluffy, about 3 minutes.
7. Add the vanilla and 2 tsps. coconut extract.
8. Blend to combine.
9. Add the eggs one at a time, blending after each addition (the mixture may separate a bit at this point).
10. Sift together 3/4 cup coconut flour, baking powder and salt.
11. Add to butter mixture and mix until thoroughly combined.
12. Add in the coconut milk and 1/2 cup shredded coconut.
13. Blend until incorporated.
14. Scoop into prepared pans and spread evenly with a spatula.
15. Bake for 35-40 minutes until cakes begin to pull away from the pans and are fully set in the center.
16. Cool for 10 minutes in the pan.
17. Remove from pan and then cool on a rack.
18. The cakes will be a little fragile so be careful handling them.
19. Place cooled cakes in the refrigerator until ready to frost and serve.
20. Frost just before serving.

Frosting Directions:

1. With an electric mixer, blend the cream cheese and 1 cup butter until smooth.
2. Add 5 tbsps. of xylitol and 1 tsp. coconut extract.

3. Bblend until light and fluffy.
4. Use 1/3 of the frosting to frost between the layers and the remaining to frost the top and the sides of the cake.
5. Toast the remaining 1/2 cup shredded coconut in the oven at 350 degrees F for 5 minutes until lightly browned.
6. Sprinkle coconut on top of the cake and along sides if desired.
7. Serve and enjoy!

Gingerbread Cupcakes

Cupcakes Ingredients:

3 cups almond flour
¼ cup unflavored whey protein powder
2 tbsp. ground ginger
1 tbsp. cocoa powder
1 tbsp. baking powder
½ tbsp.. ground cinnamon
½ tsp. ground cloves
¼ tsp. salt
½ cup butter, softened
¾ cup Swerve Sweetener
1 tbsp. molasses (optional, helps colour and flavour)
3 large eggs, room temperature
1 tsp. vanilla extract
¾ cup heavy cream mixed with water (about half of each)

Frosting Ingredients:

8 oz. cream cheese, softened
¼ cup butter, softened
6 tbsp. confectioner's Swerve Sweetener
6 tbsp. cream, room temperature
1 tsp. vanilla

Cupcakes Directions:

1. Preheat oven to 325 degrees F and line a 12 cavity muffin pan with paper liners.
2. In a large bowl, whisk together the almond flour, whey protein powder, ginger, cocoa powder, baking powder, cinnamon, cloves, and salt.
3. In another large bowl, beat butter with Swerve until light and fluffy, about 3 minutes.
4. Beat in molasses, eggs, and vanilla extract.
5. Beat in half of the almond flour mixture, then the cream/water mixture, and then the remaining almond flour mixture, until well combined. Scrape down beaters and sides of bowl as needed.
6. Divide batter among prepared muffin cups and bake 28 to 32 minutes, until lightly browned and firm to the touch.
7. Remove and let cool completely.

Frosting Directions:

1. In a large bowl, beat cream cheese with butter until smooth.
2. Beat in powdered Swerve until combined.
3. Beat in cream and vanilla until a spreadable consistency is achieved.

4. Pipe or spread onto cooled cupcakes.

Pumpkin Spice Cake

Cake Ingredients:

1 1/2 cups pumpkin puree
2 cups almond flour
1/3 cup coconut flour
1/3 cup unflavored whey protein powder
1 tbsp. baking powder
2 tsp cinnamon
1 tsp. ginger
1/2 tsp. cloves
1/4 cup butter
1/2 cup Swerve sweetener or other erythritol
3 large eggs
1 tsp. vanilla extract
1/2 tsp. stevia extract
1/4 cup almond milk

Glaze Ingredients:

1/2 cup butter
2 cups powdered Swerve Sweetener or other powdered erythritol,
sifted
1/4 cup cream, room temperature

Directions:

1. For the cake, lay down two layers of paper towel on a plate and spread out pumpkin puree. Top with another two layers of paper towel to sop up as much moisture as possible. Let dry for 20 minutes.
2. Preheat oven to 325 degrees F.
3. Grease two 8-inch round cake pans.
4. Line bottoms of pans with parchment and grease the parchment.
5. In a medium bowl, whisk together the almond flour, coconut flour, whey protein, baking powder and spices.
6. In a large bowl, beat butter, erythritol and pumpkin puree together until smooth.
7. Beat in eggs, vanilla extract, and stevia extract.
8. Beat in almond flour mixture in two additions, alternating with almond milk.
9. Divide batter evenly between prepared pans and smooth the top. Bake 40 minutes or until edges are browned and a tester inserted in the center comes out clean.
10. Let cool in pan 20 minutes, then flip out onto wire racks to cool completely.

11. For the glaze, melt butter in a saucepan over medium heat until it browns and becomes fragrant. In a medium bowl, place powdered erythritol and slowly pour in browned butter, beating to combine.
12. Add cream and beat until smooth and a spreadable consistency has been achieved.
13. To assemble, place on layer of cake on a serving plate and spread with about half of the frosting.
14. Add the second layer of cake and spread the top with half of the frosting.

Almond Cake

Ingredients:

3/4 cup butter, softened
1 cup granular Splenda or equivalent liquid Splenda
4 eggs
1/2 cup heavy cream
1 tsp. vanilla
1 1/2 cups almond flour
1/2 cup coconut flour, sifted
1/4 tsp. salt *
2 tsps. baking powder
1 cup water, optional

Directions:

1. Put all of the ingredients in a medium to large mixing bowl. Beat with an electric mixer until well blended and creamy. If the batter is too stiff, you can beat in up to 1 cup of water to thin it a little.
2. Spread in a greased 9x13" pan.
3. Bake at 350 degrees for 30-35 minutes until golden and firm to the touch.
4. Cool completely before serving.
5. Store in the refrigerator.

Muffins

Low Carb Banana Muffins

Ingredients:

3/4 cup almond meal
2 tbsps. coconut flour
2 tbsp. chia seeds
1 tsp. cinnamon
1/4 tsp. salt
1/2 tsp. baking soda
1 large ripe banana, mashed
1 egg
1 tbsp. coconut oil, melted
2 tbsp. unsweetened almond milk
1/2 tsp. vanilla extract
1/4 cup chopped pecans

Directions:

1. Preheat oven to 350 degrees and grease a mini-muffin pan.
2. Combine almond meal, coconut flour, chia seeds, cinnamon, salt and baking soda in a large bowl.
3. Whisk together remaining ingredients in a small bowl.
4. Add the wet ingredients to the dry and stir to combine.
5. Fold nuts into the batter until evenly distributed.
6. Spoon batter into mini-muffin pan and bake for about 15 minutes until tops start to turn golden brown.
7. Remove from oven and let cool for a few minutes before transferring to a cooling rack.
8. Serve and enjoy!

Sugar Free Jalapeno and Cheddar Muffins

Ingredients:

2 cups finely riced, raw cauliflower
2 tbsp. minced jalapeno
2 eggs, beaten
2 tbsp. melted butter
1/3 cup grated parmesan cheese
1 cup grated mozzarella cheese
1 cup grated cheddar cheese
1 tbsp. dried onion flakes
¼ tsp. salt
¼ tsp. black pepper
½ tsp. garlic powder
½ tsp. baking powder
¼ cup coconut flour

Directions:

1. Preheat oven to 375 degrees F.
2. Combine the cauliflower, jalapeno, eggs, add melted butter in a medium bowl.
3. Add the grated cheeses and mix well.
4. Stir in the onion flakes, salt, pepper, garlic powder, baking powder and coconut flour until thoroughly combined.
5. Divide the batter evenly between 12 greased muffin cups.
6. Bake for 30 minutes or until golden brown.
7. Turn off the oven and leave the muffins inside for about an hour.
8. Remove from the oven.
9. Cool on a wire rack.
10. Serve and enjoy!

Low Carb Pumpkin Muffins

Ingredients:

2 cups pumpkin puree
1 cup almond meal
⅔ cup coconut flour
1 cup sweetener
1 tablespoon pumpkin spice
1½ teaspoons cinnamon
2 teaspoons vanilla
½ teaspoon salt
½ teaspoon baking soda
2 eggs

Directions:

1. Preheat oven to 350.
2. Line muffin pan with liners.
3. In large bowl, beat pumpkin, sweetener and eggs, until fluffy.
4. Beat in the remaining ingredients until fully combined.
5. Scoop batter into prepared muffin pan and bake for 30-35 minutes or until tooth pick (or knife) comes out clean.
6. Cool in pan on a rack five minutes, then transfer muffins from pan to rack and let cool for additional 10 minutes.

Sugar Free Poppy Seed Muffins

Ingredients:

1 cup almond flour
1/2 cup golden flax meal
1 tsp. baking powder
1/8 tsp. salt
1 tsp. poppy seeds
1 cup granular Splenda
2 tbsp. butter
1 tsp. pure lemon extract
1 tsp. vanilla
2 tbsps. heavy cream
2 tbsps. water
2 eggs

Directions:

1. Preheat oven to 350 degrees F.
2. Line 6 muffin cups with liners.
3. In a small bowl,, stir together the almond flour, flax meal, baking powder, salt, poppy seeds and granular Splenda, if using.
4. In a medium microwave-safe bowl, melt the butter in the microwave.
5. Stir in the Splenda, lemon extract, cream and water.
6. Add the dry ingredients and the eggs to the butter mixture.
7. Stir with a wooden spoon until well blended.
8. Fill muffin cups evenly with the batter.
9. Bake 15-20 minutes, until the tops are golden brown.
10. Cool 5 minutes on a rack before removing from the pan.
11. Serve and enjoy!

No Sugar Strawberry Lemon Muffins

Ingredients:

6 eggs
2¼ cups almond flour
1 cup strawberries, chopped
¼ cup coconut flour
¼ cup sweetener
¼ cup sugar free artificial honey
1 tsp. vanilla
½ teaspoon salt
2 tbsp. butter
1 tsp. baking soda

Streusel Ingredients:

¼ cup almond flour
⅓ cup chopped pecans (or any other nuts)
1 tbsp. sugar free honey
2 tbsp. sweetener
2 tbsp. butter, softened
½ tsp. cinnamon

Directions:

1. Preheat oven to 350 degrees F.
2. Line a 12-cup muffin tin with paper liners.
3. In a large mixing bowl combine almond flour, coconut flour, sweetener, baking soda and salt.
4. Slowly add in eggs, honey, butter and vanilla.
5. Make sure all ingredients are blended thoroughly.
6. Fold in strawberries, making sure not to puree them.
7. In a separate bowl, mix streusel ingredients and set aside.
8. Pour batter evenly among the muffin liners.
9. Lightly sprinkle with streusel topping.
10. Bake for 25-30 minutes.

Low Carb Apple Cinnamon Muffins

Ingredients:

2 cups almond flour
1 cup walnuts, chopped
2 tbsp. ground flax seeds
2 tsp. baking powder
1 tbsp. cinnamon
1⁄2 tsp. salt
2 large eggs, beaten
1 cup unsweetened applesauce
1⁄2 cup coconut oil, melted
1⁄2 cup sour cream

Directions:

1. Preheat oven to 325 degrees F.
2. Line muffin tins with baking cups.
3. Combine all dry ingredients.
4. In a separate bowl, combine all wet ingredients.
5. Stir wet ingredients into dry ingredients until well blended.
6. Spoon evenly into baking cups.
7. Bake muffins 30 minutes or until a toothpick comes out clean.
8. Cool for 20 minutes.
9. Serve and enjoy!

Sugar Free Blueberry Muffins

Ingredients:

Vegetable oil cooking spray
2 tablespoons wheat (or oat) bran and 1 tablespoon soy flour, mixed together
1 cup soy flour
1/2 cup sugar substitute
1 tsp. baking powder
2 eggs
1/2 cup heavy cream
1/3 cup club soda
1/2 cup blueberries

Directions:

1. Preheat oven to 375 degrees F.
2. Spray a 6-cup muffin tin with vegetable oil cooking spray.
3. Evenly sprinkle the pan with the wheat bran and soy flour mix, being careful to coat the sides of the cups also; this will prevent sticking.
4. In a bowl using a wire whisk, mix all the remaining ingredients, except the blueberries, until well blended.
5. Fold in the blueberries and fill the 6 muffin cups evenly with the batter.
6. Place on the center rack of the oven and bake for 20 to 25 minutes, or until the tops turn golden brown and a toothpick stuck in the center comes out clean.
7. from oven and let cool.
8. Serve and enjoy!

No Sugar Sweet Potato Muffins

Ingredients:

3/4 cup almond meal
1 tsp. baking soda
1/4 tsp. salt
Spices: 1 tsp. ground cinnamon
1/2 tsp. ground cardamom
1/4 tsp. ground cloves
1/4 tsp. anise powder
2/3 cup coconut cream
3 tbsps. almond butter
4 large eggs, at room temperature
Zest of 1 orange
2 tsps. vanilla extract
1 tablespoon apple cider vinegar
1 cup raw grated sweet potato
1/2 cup sugar substitute

Directions:

1. Preheat oven to 350 degrees F.
2. Line a muffin tin with muffin liners.
3. In a medium bowl, mix almond meal, baking soda, salt, and spices.
4. Mix well.
5. Add the coconut butter and almond butter and mix well again.
6. Add the eggs, zest, vanilla, vinegar, sweet potato, and sweetener.
7. Mix until smooth.
8. Sweeten to taste.
9. Fill muffin cups about 3/4 full with batter.
10. Bake 22 - 28 minutes, or until a wooden toothpick comes out clean.

Chocolate Chip and Fig Muffins

Ingredients:

1 cup unsalted sunflower seed butter (sunbutter)
2 ripe bananas
2 eggs
1/2 tsp. baking soda
1/2 tsp. vanilla
1/8 tsp. salt
1/2 cup diabetic chocolate chips
1/2 cup chopped dried figs (about 7 figs)

Directions:

1. Preheat oven to 400 degrees F.
2. Line a muffin pan with muffin liners.
3. In a food processor or blender, combine the sunbutter, bananas, eggs, vanilla, baking soda, and salt.
4. Puree until smooth.
5. Fold in the chocolate chips and figs until evenly distributed.
6. Spoon the batter into the muffin liners until they are about 3/4 of the way full.
7. Bake for 15 to 20 minutes, until golden on top and a toothpick comes out clean when inserted into the middle.
8. Cool on a wire rack.
9. Serve and enjoy!

Sugar Free English Muffins

Ingredients:

1 egg
1 tbsp. coconut flour
1 tsp. psyllium husk powder
1 tbsp. water
pinch of baking powder
pinch of salt

Directions:

1. Whisk together the egg, olive oil and water in a mug or a small microwavable bowl or ramekin
2. Add the coconut flour, psyllium husk, baking powder and salt, and whisk until there are no lumps
3. Microwave on high for about 1 ½ - 2 minutes, until it is cooked through.
4. Serve and enjoy!

Chocolate Chocolate Chip Muffins

Ingredients:

1 cup ground almonds
1/2 cup sugar-free cocoa powder
4 tbsp. Truvia
1 tbsp. baking powder
1 tbsp. sugar-free vanilla extract
1 small pinch of salt
2 large eggs
1/2 cup (120ml / 4oz) single cream
1 oz. sugar-free chocolate chips

Directions:

1. Line a muffin tin with muffin cups.
2. Preheat oven to 375 degrees F.
3. Mix all dry ingredients together thoroughly.
4. Lightly beat eggs.
5. Add vanilla extract and cream and combine.
6. Add wet ingredients to dry ingredients and mix well until smooth.
7. Fold in chocolate chips.
8. Spoon mixture into muffin cups.
9. Bake for 30-40 minutes.
10. Cool on a wire rack.
11. Serve and enjoy!

Bacon Egg and Cheese Muffins

Ingredients:

2/3 cup cottage cheese
1/2 cup grated parmesan cheese
1/4 cup coconut flour
2/3 cup almond flour
1 tsp. baking powder
1/2 tsp. salt
3 tbsps. water
5 eggs, beaten
3 strips bacon
1/2 cup cheddar cheese, shredded

Directions:

1. Cook the bacon until crisp.
2. Drain on a paper towel until cool.
3. Crumble bacon into small pieces in a bowl.
4. Preheat oven to 400 F.
5. Spray a muffin tin with nonstick cooking spray.
6. In mixing bowl, combine cottage cheese, parmesan cheese, coconut flour, almond meal, baking powder, salt, water, and beaten egg.
7. Mix in crumbled bacon and cheddar cheese.
8. Fill muffin cups 3/4 full.
9. Sprinkle muffin tops with additional shredded cheddar cheese.
10. Bake 25 -30 minutes, until muffins are firm and lightly browned.
11. Serve and enjoy!

Sugar Free Zucchini and Cheese Muffins

Ingredients:

4 eggs
1 1/2 cups grated zucchini
1/4 cup melted butter
1/4 cup water
1/4 tsp. salt
1/3 cup coconut flour
1/4 tsp. baking soda
1/2 cup grated parmesan cheese
1 tbsp. dried oregano
1 tbsp. thyme, fresh and chopped
1/4 cup cheddar cheese, grated

Directions:

1. Preheat the oven to 400 degrees F.
2. Spray a muffin tin with non-stick cooking spray.
3. Combine the eggs, butter, water and salt with a hand blender.
4. Add the coconut flour and baking soda and mix well.
5. Add in the zucchini, thyme and oregano.
6. Add in the Parmesan cheese and blend.
7. Put the mixture into muffin tin and sprinkle the grated cheddar cheese on top.
8. Bake for 13-15 minutes until golden on top and firm.
9. Serve and enjoy!

No Sugar Spinach Egg Muffins

Ingredients:

1 egg
1 cup egg white
1 dash black pepper
1 tsp red or cayenne pepper
1/4 cup crumbled feta cheese
3/4 cup baby spinach
1/4 tsp. garlic powder

Directions:

1. Preheat oven to 350 degrees F.
2. Mix together all ingredients except feta cheese and black pepper.
3. Pour into greased muffin tins,
4. fill 2/3 full, and top with feta cheese and pepper.
5. Bake for 15-20 minutes.
6. Cool on a wire rack.
7. Serve and enjoy!

Low Carb Cornbread Muffins

Ingredients:

1 ½ cups almond flour
1/4 tsp. salt
1/2 tsp. garlic powder
2 tbsp. baking powder, aluminum free
1/3 cup cheddar cheese, shredded
2 large eggs, beaten
1/3 cup sour cream
4 tbsp. melted butter

Directions:

1. Preheat oven to 400 degrees F.
2. Spray muffin pan with nonstick cooking spray or line with muffin cups.
3. Set aside.
4. Mix almond flour, salt, garlic powder, & baking powder very well.
5. Add in cheese & mix evenly.
6. In a separate bowl or large measuring cup, melt butter in the microwave, set aside.
7. In another bowl, mix eggs and sour cream together.
8. Using a hand mixer, add eggs and sour cream to the dry ingredients until well mixed.
9. Add melted butter & continue mixing.
10. Spoon 2 heaping tablespoons into each muffin cup.
11. bake for 10 to 12 minutes.
12. Cool on a wire rack.
13. Serve and enjoy!

Sugar Free Flax Muffins

Ingredients:

2 cups flax seed meal
5 eggs, separated
5 tbsp. olive oil
1 tbsp. baking soda
1 tsp. salt
1/2 cup water
3 packets Stevia or Truvia

Directions:

1. Preheat oven to 350 degrees F.
2. If needed, grind flaxseed using food processor or coffee grinder into meal.
3. In a bowl, mix together baking soda, stevia, and salt.
4. whisk to combine dry ingredients.
5. In a separate bowl, mix egg yolks, olive oil, and water.
6. Add to flax meal tomixture.
7. In another bowl whisk or beat egg whites to soft peaks.
8. Gently fold egg whites into flax mixture, 1/3 at a time to keep the batter light and fluffy.
9. Spray muffin tin with cooking spray.
10. Fill each cup 2/3 full.
11. Bake for 12-15 minutes; until a toothpick comes out clean.
12. Cool muffins on a wire rack.
13. Serve and enjoy!

Low Carb Cranberry Muffins

Ingredients:

1 cup whole fresh cranberries
1 ¼ cup flax seed meal
1 tsp. baking powder
3 tbsp. cinnamon
1 tsp nutmeg
1/2 tsp. salt
1/2 cup Splenda
4 eggs
¼ cup olive oil
1/2 cup sugar free vanilla syrup
1 tbsp. vanilla

Directions:

1. Preheat oven to 350 degrees F.
2. Liberally butter muffin tins, for up to 15 muffins. Muffin liners are not recommended for this recipe because they stick.
3. Pour boiling water over cranberries and let sit for 5 minutes.
4. mix wet ingredients and dry ingredients separately except for the cranberries.
5. Combine the wet and dry ingredients.
6. let mixture stand for about 10 minutes to thicken a bit.
7. Fold in cranberries.
8. Fill each muffin cup 3/4 full.
9. Bake for about 17 minutes or until toothpick comes out clean.
10. Let cool.
11. Serve and enjoy!

Sugar Free Gingerbread Cream Cheese Muffins

Ingredients:

8 oz. cream cheese, softened
2 eggs
3 tbsp. unsweetened almond milk
2 tsp. molasses (optional)
16 drops stevia extract
1 1/2 cup almond flour
1/4 cup vanilla whey protein powder
1/4 cup granulated erythritol
2 tsp. baking powder
1/2 tsp. baking soda
1 tsp. ground cinnamon
1 tsp. ground ginger
1/2 tsp. ground cloves
1/4 tsp. salt

Directions:

1. Preheat oven to 325 degrees F.
2. Line a 12-muffin pan with muffin liners.
3. In a large bowl, beat cream cheese with electric mixer until smooth.
4. Add eggs, one at a time, and beat until combined, scraping down sides of bowl and beaters as needed.
5. Add almond milk, molasses and stevia extract and beat until just incorporated.
6. In a medium bowl, stir together almond flour, whey powder, erythritol, baking powder, baking soda, spices and salt.
7. Add to wet ingredients and beat until just incorporated, being careful not to overmix.
8. Spoon batter into prepared muffin cups and bake for 20-25 minutes, or until golden brown.
9. Let cool.
10. Serve and enjoy!

Low Carb Vanilla Pear Muffins

Ingredients:

2 ¼ cups gluten-free bake mix
2 tsp. baking powder
½ tsp. baking soda
½ tsp. salt
3 eggs
Liquid sugar substitute equal to 2/3 cup
  sugar
1/3 cup olive oil
1/4 cup granulated erythritol
21/4 tsp unflavored gelatin
2 tsp. vanilla extract
1/2 cup milk
1 1/4 cups diced pears

Directions:

1. Preheat oven to 425 degrees F.
2. Grease 12 muffin cups.
3. In a bowl, combine bake mix, baking powder, baking soda and salt.
4. In food processor, process eggs.
5. Add liquid sugar substitute, milk, olive oil, erythritol, gelatin and vanilla.
6. Mix until combined.
7. Add half dry ingredients and half milk.
8. Mix again.
9. Repeat, scraping sides once or twice.
10. Fold pears into muffin batter.
11. Fill muffin cups 3/4 full.
12. Place in oven and immediately reduce oven temperature to 400 degrees F.
13. Bake 25 minutes, or until toothpick inserted in a muffin comes out clean.
14. Let cool.
15. Serve and enjoy!

Low Carb Carrot Muffins

Ingredients:

2 cups ground almond meal
2 tbsps. ground flaxseed
½ tsp. sea salt
1 tsp. baking powder
2 tsps. ground cinnamon
1 tsp. ground cloves
1 cup chopped pecans
Sugar substitute equivalent to ½ cup sugar
1 cup shredded carrots
2 tbsps. orange zest
¼ cup sour cream? or coconut milk
2 eggs
¼ cup extra-light olive oil
1/2 cup raisins

Directions:

1. Preheat oven to 325 degrees F.
2. Grease muffin tin with oil.
3. Mix almond meal, flaxseed, salt, baking powder, cinnamon, nutmeg, cloves, pecans, and sweetener in bowl and mix.
4. Mix in carrots, orange zest, sour cream or coconut milk, eggs, oil, optional raisins and blend ingredients thoroughly.
5. Spoon mixture into muffin pan (fill each about ½ full).
6. Bake for 40 minutes or until toothpick emerges dry.
7. Cool and remove.
8. Serve and enjoy!

Sugar Free Spinach Muffins

Wet ingredients:

4 eggs
1/4 cup softened butter or margarine
1/3 cup mayonnaise
1 handful of fresh spinach leaves
1/3 cup green onions, chopped

Dry ingredients:

2 cups almond flour
1/2 cup flax seed meal
2 tsp baking powder
1 tsp baking soda
1/2 tsp guar gum
1/2 tsp seasoning salt
1 cup shredded sharp cheddar cheese
1/3 cup parmesano regiano, grated
1/2 cup bacon bits

Directions:

1. Preheat oven to 350 degrees F.
2. Line a muffin tin with paper liners.
3. In a blender, combine the wet ingredients.
4. In another bowl combine the dry ingredients and use a whisk to combine.
5. Stir together wet and dry ingredients.
6. Make sure everything is well combined.
7. Let the batter sit for a couple of minutes to thicken a bit.
8. Divide the batter equally among your muffin cups.
9. Bake for about 17 - 25 minutes or until golden brown and a toothpick inserted in the middle comes out clean.
10. Serve and enjoy!

Sugar Free Blackberry Muffins

Ingredients:

Vegetable oil cooking spray
2 tbsps. oat bran and 1 tablespoon soy flour, mixed together
1 cup soy flour
1/2 cup sugar substitute
1 tsp. baking powder
2 eggs
1/2 cup heavy cream
1/3 cup club soda
1/2 cup blackberries

Directions:

1. Preheat oven to 375 degrees F.
2. Spray a 6-cup muffin tin with vegetable oil cooking spray.
3. Evenly sprinkle the pan with the wheat bran and soy flour mix, being careful to coat the sides of the cups also; this will prevent sticking.
4. In a bowl using a wire whisk, mix all the remaining ingredients, except the blackberries, until well blended.
5. Fold in the blackberries and fill the 6 muffin cups evenly with the batter.
6. Place on the center rack of the oven and bake for 20 to 25 minutes, or until the tops turn golden brown and a toothpick stuck in the center comes out clean.
7. Remove from oven and let cool.
8. Serve and enjoy!

Carb Counter Coconut Muffins

Ingredients:

6 eggs
4 tbsp. melted butter
4 tbsp. melted coconut oil
1/4 cup almond milk
1.5 tbsp. vanilla extract
1/2 cup sugar substitute, granulated
2/3 cup coconut flour
1 tsp. baking powder
1/2 tsp. salt

Directions:

1. Preheat the oven to 375 degrees F.
2. Whisk together the eggs, butter, coconut oil, almond milk, vanilla extract, and sugar substitute.
3. In another bowl, whisk together the coconut flour, baking powder, and salt.
4. Slowly add the coconut flour to the wet ingredients and stir to incorporate. The batter will be thick.
5. Pour into prepared standard muffin tin.
6. Bake for 20-25 minutes until cooked through.

About the Author

Laura Sommers is **The Recipe Lady!**

She is a loving wife and mother who lives on a small farm in Baltimore County, Maryland and has a passion for all things domestic especially when it comes to saving money. She has a profitable eBay business and is a couponing addict. Follow her tips and tricks to learn how to make delicious meals on a budget, save money or to learn the latest life hack!

Visit her Amazon Author Page to see her latest books:

amazon.com/author/laurasommers

Visit the Recipe Lady's blog for even more great recipes:

http://the-recipe-lady.blogspot.com/

Follow the Recipe Lady on **Pinterest**:

http://pinterest.com/therecipelady1

Other Books by Laura Sommers

Egg Salad Recipes

The Chip Dip Cookbook

Zucchini Recipes

Salsa recipes

Traditional Vermont Recipes

Recipe Hacks for Dry Onion Soup Mix

Made in the USA
Monee, IL
10 January 2020